HISPANIC LEADERS OF COURAGE

SYLVIA MENDEZ

EZRA E. KNOPP

PowerKiDS press.

Published in 2026 by The Rosen Publishing Group, Inc.
2544 Clinton Street, Buffalo, NY 14224

First Edition

Editor: Therese Shea
Book Design: Michael Flynn

Photo Credits: Cover, pp. 1, 5 Nature and Science/Alamy Stock Photo; (series background) Sergei Mishchenko/Shutterstock.com; p. 7 (aerial view) Matt Gush/Shutterstock.com; p. 7 (map) drdefend/Shutterstock.com; p. 9 https://en.wikipedia.org/wiki/Sylvia_Mendez#/media/File:Sylvia_Mendez.jpg; p. 11 courtesy of Orange County Public Library; p. 13 Okyela/Shutterstock.com; p. 15 https://commons.wikimedia.org/wiki/File:Taos_County,_New_Mexico._The_hot_lunch,_school_at_Penasco._Children_pay_about_1_cent_daily_for_thi_._._._-_NARA_-_521840.jpg; p. 17 https://commons.wikimedia.org/wiki/File:Gonzalo_and_Felicitas_Mendez_Statue.jpg; p. 19 UPI/Alamy Stock Photo; p. 21 Photo Win1/Shutterstock.com.

Library of Congress Cataloging-in-Publication Data

Names: Knopp, Ezra E., author.
Title: Sylvia Mendez / Ezra E. Knopp.
Description: Buffalo : PowerKids Press, 2025. | Series: Hispanic leaders of courage | Includes bibliographical references and index.
Identifiers: LCCN 2024044645 (print) | LCCN 2024044646 (ebook) | ISBN 9781499451016 (library binding) | ISBN 9781499451009 (paperback) | ISBN 9781499451023 (ebook)
Subjects: LCSH: Mendez, Sylvia, 1963- | School integration–California–Orange County–Juvenile literature. | Mexican Americans–Segregation–California–Orange County–History–Juvenile literature. | Mexican American women–California–Biography–Juvenile literature. | Puerto Rican women–California–Biography–Juvenile literature. | Mexican Americans–California–Social conditions–20th century–Juvenile literature. | Civil rights workers–United States–Biography–Juvenile literature.
Classification: LCC LC214.22.C2 K567 2025 (print) | LCC LC214.22.C2 (ebook) | DDC 379.2/63092 [B]–dc23/eng/20241007
LC record available at https://lccn.loc.gov/2024044645

LC ebook record available at https://lccn.loc.gov/2024044646

Manufactured in China

Some of the images in this book illustrate individuals who are models. The depictions do not imply actual situations or events.

CPSIA Compliance Information: Batch #QSPK26. For Further Information contact Rosen Publishing at 1-800-237-9932.

CONTENTS

Against Injustice

Many people face **injustice**. Some try to change that injustice. It's often hard to do. Sylvia Mendez was a young girl when she faced **discrimination** at school. This started her work as an **activist**. She fights for equal rights for children.

Childhood

Sylvia Mendez was born in Santa Ana, California, in 1936. Her father, Gonzalo, was from Mexico. Her mother, Felicitas, was from Puerto Rico. When Sylvia was young, they moved to a farm in Westminster in Orange County, California. Sylvia's **siblings**, aunt, and cousins lived there too.

CALIFORNIA
WESTMINSTER

School Time

When she was eight, Sylvia's parents wanted her to go to school. The closest one was 17th Street School. Gonzalo had gone there when he was young. Sylvia's Aunt Sally took her children and the Mendez children to the school to sign them up.

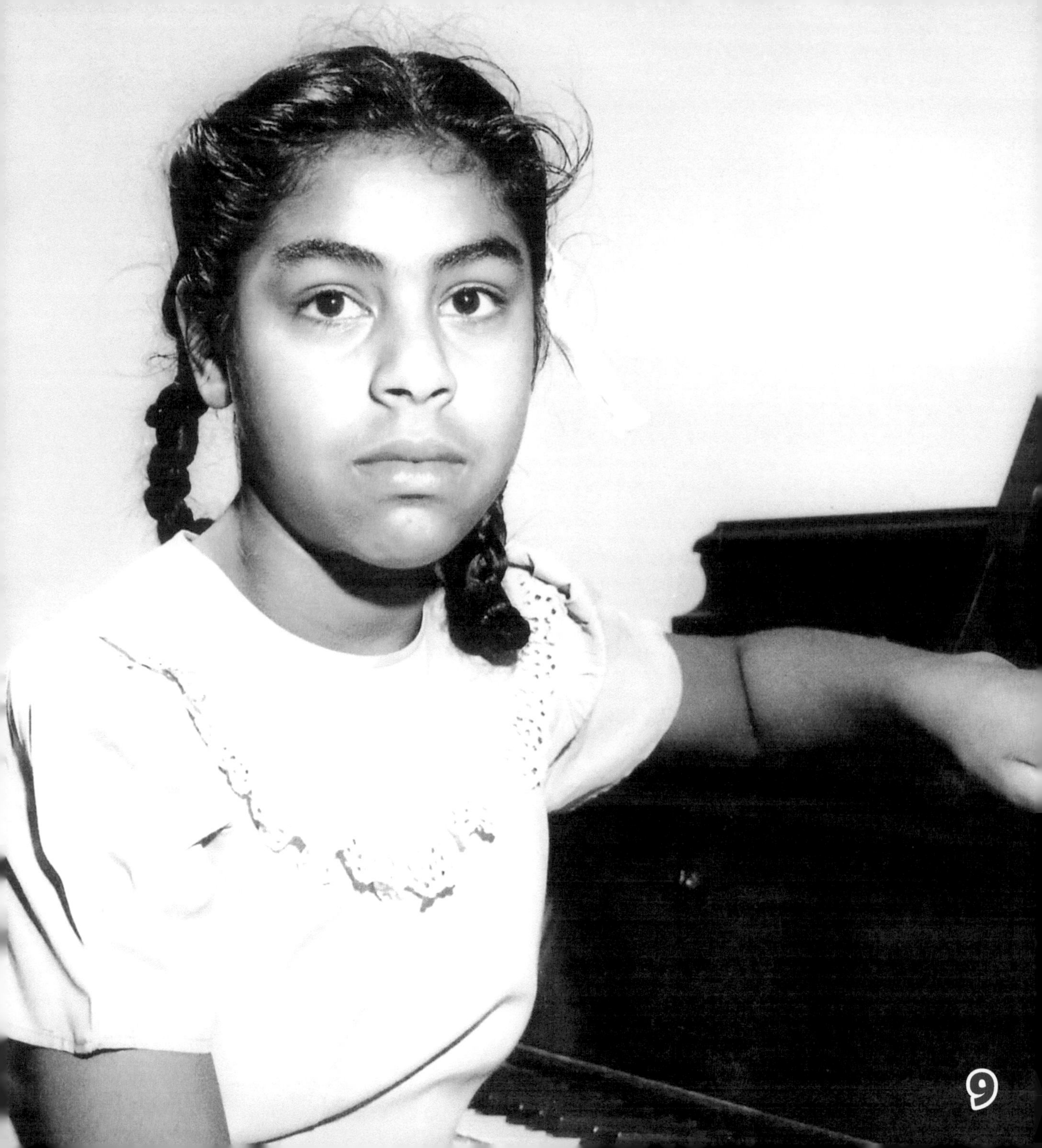

The school told Aunt Sally that her children could attend. Sylvia and her brothers could not. Sylvia's cousins had lighter skin. They didn't have a **Hispanic** last name like the Mendez children had. Sylvia and her brothers were told to go to Hoover Elementary, a school for Mexican American children.

Hoover School, 7th and 8th grades, 1944

"Separate but Equal"

At that time, schools in Orange County were **segregated**. Mexican American children went to separate schools. In 1896, the U.S. Supreme Court, the highest court, had ruled that "separate but equal" schools and services were allowed under the U.S. Constitution, the nation's highest law.

WHITES ONLY

"Separate but equal" meant separate schools for children of different races and **ethnicities** in many places. But the schools weren't often equal. Sylvia's parents tried talking to 17th Street School officials. The officials offered to let in the Mendez children if no other Mexican Americans were let in. The family didn't agree.

lunch at school for Mexican American children in New Mexico, 1941

The Court Case

In 1945, the Mendez family and others **sued** the Westminster school **district** and several other districts. They won the court case and another that followed. The judges said school segregation was against the Constitution. In 1948, Sylvia started classes at 17th Street School. Some children there were unkind to her, but Sylvia was brave.

statue of Sylvia's parents in Westminster, California

Later Life

Sylvia worked hard in school and went on to college. She worked as a nurse for 30 years. She continues to tell others her story. She speaks out about equality in schools. In 2011, President Barack Obama gave Sylvia the Presidential Medal of Freedom for her hard work.

A Win for All

The court case win for the Mendez family wasn't just a win for California. It helped win another court case in 1954. This one, *Brown v. Board of Education,* made segregation in schools illegal everywhere in the United States. The bravery of Sylvia and her family helped all American children!

Sylvia's Fight for Her Rights

1936

Sylvia Mendez is born in Santa Ana, California.

1944

Sylvia and her brothers are not allowed to attend a school because they're Mexican American.

1945

The Mendez family and others sue Orange County school districts that segregate children.

1946

Courts rule that school segregation is against the Constitution.

1948

Sylvia and other Mexican American children attend 17th Street School.

2011

President Barack Obama gives Sylvia the Presidential Medal of Freedom.

GLOSSARY

activist: A person who uses or supports strong actions to help make changes in politics or society.

discrimination: Unfairly treating people unequally because of their race, ethnicity, or beliefs.

district: An area with a special feature or government.

ethnicity: A part of a person's identity based on where they or their family comes from.

Hispanic: One who came from or whose family came from an area where Spanish is spoken, especially from Latin America.

injustice: Unfairness.

segregate: To separate people of different races by force or law.

sibling: A brother or sister.

sue: To use a legal method to get a court to force a person, company, or organization that has treated you unfairly or harmed you to do something.

FOR MORE INFORMATION

BOOKS

Gonzales, Leticia. *The Untold Story of Sylvia Mendez: School Desegregation Pioneer.* North Mankato, MN: Capstone Press, 2023.

Weston, Margeaux. *Brown v. Board of Education: A Day That Changed America.* North Mankato, MN: Capstone Press, 2022.

WEBSITES

Meet the Hero: Sylvia Mendez
www.lowellmilkencenter.org/programs/projects/view/sylvia-mendez/hero
Read more about this courageous leader.

Presidential Medal of Freedom Recipient: Sylvia Mendez
www.docsteach.org/documents/document/presidential-medal-of-freedom-sylvia-mendez
Watch a video about Sylvia and her fight for equal rights.

INDEX